THE PLANETARY SOCIETY

ASTEROIDS AND COMETS

ORBITING SPACE ROCKS

Bruce Betts, PhD

Lerner Publications ◆ Minneapolis

THE PLANETS AND MOONS IN OUR SOLAR SYSTEM ARE OUT OF THIS WORLD. Some are hotter than an oven, and some are much colder than a freezer. Some are small and rocky, while others are huge and mostly made of gas. As you explore these worlds, you'll discover giant canyons, active volcanoes, strange kinds of ice, storms bigger than Earth, and much more.

The Planetary Society® empowers people around the world to advance space science and exploration. On behalf of The Planetary Society®, including our tens of thousands of members, here's wishing you the joy of discovery.

Onward,

Bill Nye

Bill Nye
CEO, The Planetary Society®

Table of Contents

CHAPTER 1

SMALL OBJECTS OF THE SOLAR SYSTEM

The Sun is the center of our solar system. Our solar system is everything that orbits, or goes around, the Sun. This includes asteroids and comets.

Asteroids are rocky objects. Most are found in the asteroid belt. Comets are icy objects. They are often far from the Sun.

A comet as seen from Earth in 2020

ASTEROIDS FAST FACTS

Size	About 33 feet to 330 miles (10 m to 530 km) long
Distance from Earth	Varies per asteroid
Length of day	A few hours to several Earth days
Length of year	Less than one Earth year to a few Earth years

COMETS FAST FACTS

Size	About 1 to 80 miles (1.6 to 130 km) wide
Distance from Earth	Mostly far out in the solar system but varies per comet
Length of day	A few hours to several Earth days
Length of year	About three and a half Earth years to a few hundred thousand Earth years

Rocks in Space

Asteroids range in size. They are at least 33 feet (10 m) wide and can be up to a few hundred miles wide. That's between the size of a small house and a small country.

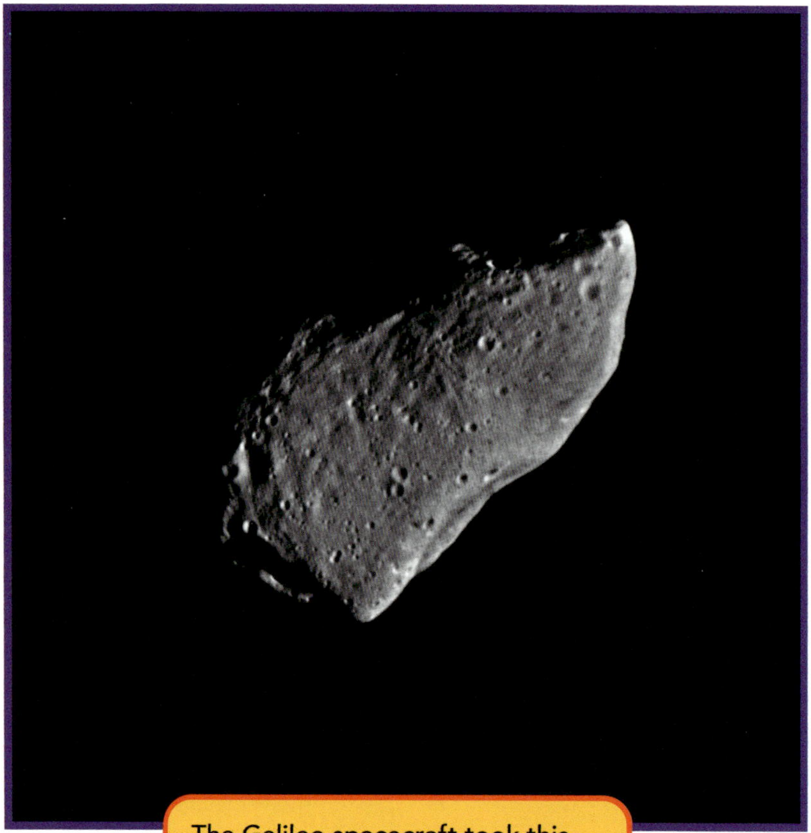

The Galileo spacecraft took this picture of asteroid Gaspra in 1991.

Which Is Bigger?
Asteroids are small compared to moons and planets. If you squished all the asteroids in the solar system into a ball, it would be smaller than Earth's Moon.

The asteroid belt is between Mars and Jupiter. Millions of objects are there. The objects are spread over a huge area. This means the belt is mostly empty space.

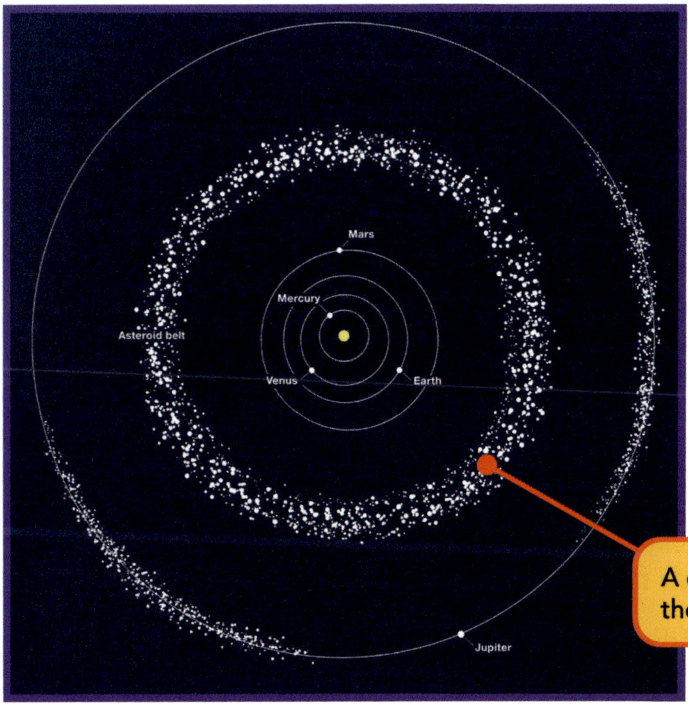

A diagram of the asteroid belt

Asteroids come in many shapes and sizes.

Large objects such as planets are round like a ball. Their gravity pulls them into ball shapes. Gravity is the force that holds you down on Earth. Asteroids are not big enough for their gravity to make them round.

Asteroids look mostly gray. Most are made of different kinds of rocks. But some are made of metal.

Some asteroids are piles of rocks held together by gravity. Others are solid rock or metal. Most are alone, but some travel in pairs.

Images of asteroid Dinkinesh (*the larger object*) and its moon, Selam

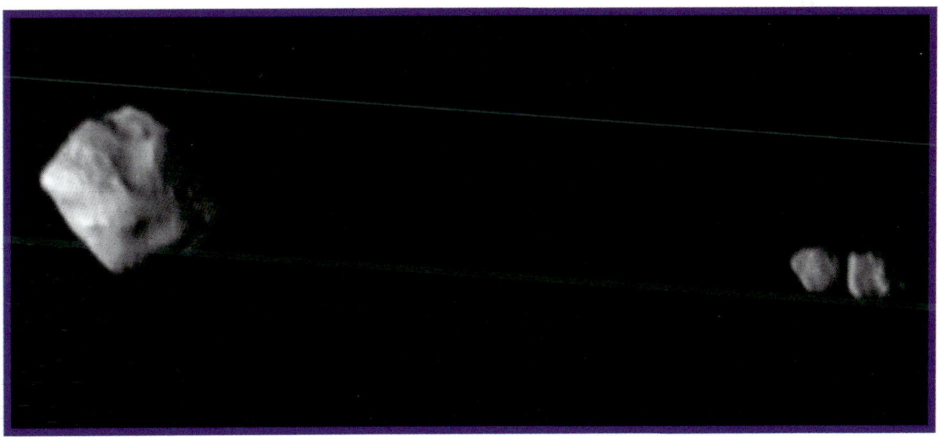

Meteors

Meteoroids are smaller space rocks than asteroids. They often hit Earth's atmosphere at high speeds. The rocks get very hot and start to burn up.

The burning of these rocks creates a streak of light called a meteor. They are also called shooting stars. You can sometimes see them in the night sky.

A meteor as seen from Earth

Scientists collect a meteorite in Antarctica.

Meteoroids will mostly burn up in the atmosphere. The rocks that don't burn up hit the ground. These rocks are meteorites.

CHAPTER 2

EXPLORING ASTEROIDS

Spacecraft missions have given us closer views of asteroids. Some have even brought back small pieces of the space rocks to Earth.

The Galileo spacecraft took a picture of asteroid Gaspra in 1991. It was the first close-up picture of an asteroid. Galileo also flew by asteroid Ida in 1993 and found the first asteroid moon.

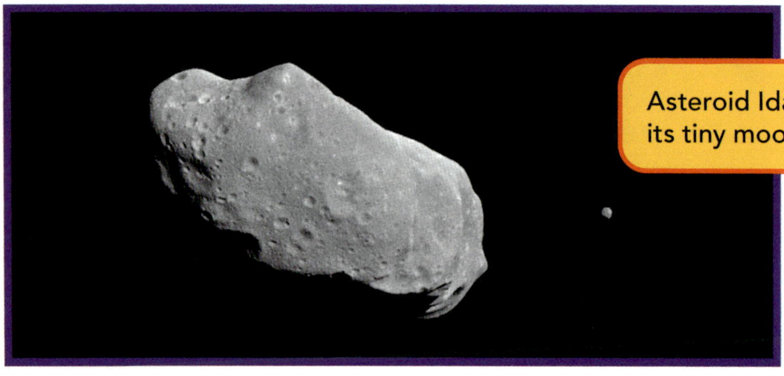

Asteroid Ida (*left*) and its tiny moon, Dactyl

NEAR Shoemaker left Earth in 1996. It was the first spacecraft to orbit and land on an asteroid. It flew by asteroid Mathilde on its way to asteroid Eros. Then it orbited Eros for about a year.

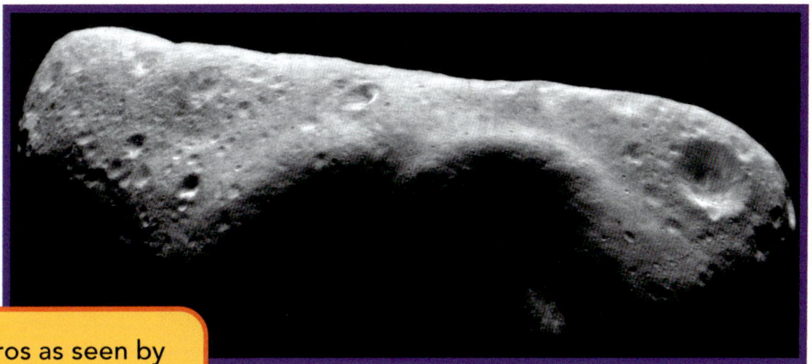

Asteroid Eros as seen by NEAR Shoemaker in 2000

This drawing shows NEAR Shoemaker with Eros.

Choosing Names
The person or people who discover an asteroid choose its name. A group of scientists must approve the name.

The Hayabusa and Hayabusa2 missions explored asteroids Itokawa and Ryugu. They brought back some dirt to Earth.

Asteroid Itokawa

Asteroid Ryugu

Asteroid Vesta as seen by Dawn

Dwarf planet Ceres in color

The Dawn spacecraft visited the large asteroid Vesta in 2011. Vesta is more than 300 miles (480 km) wide.

Dawn then visited the dwarf planet Ceres in 2015. Ceres is the largest object in the asteroid belt.

OSIRIS-REx left Earth in 2016. It orbited asteroid Bennu for more than two years. The spacecraft brought samples back to Earth in 2023. It will study asteroid Apophis in 2029.

Asteroid Bennu (*left*) and rocks on the surface of Bennu (*bottom*)

DART Mission

Humans one day may need to change the orbit of an asteroid so it does not hit Earth. The DART mission was the first test of doing this. The spacecraft was slammed into asteroid Dimorphos to change its orbit in 2022.

The asteroid was never going to hit Earth. This test was practice to learn how to protect Earth if needed.

Asteroid Dimorphos before being hit by DART in 2022

CHAPTER 3

DIRTY SNOWBALLS IN SPACE

Comets are made of ices, dust, and rocks. They are giant, dirty snowballs in space. Their size ranges from about that of a small city to that of a large city.

Comets are often very far from the Sun. They are usually too far away to see from Earth. But comets travel closer to the Sun as they go around it. That is when we get a chance to see them.

A comet as seen from Earth in 2020

Some comets go around the Sun in less than one hundred years. Others can take hundreds of thousands of years to go around the Sun.

When comets are far from the Sun, they are very cold. Their ices stay frozen. When they get closer to the Sun, the heat warms them up. The warming ice becomes a gas. The gas pushes some of the dirt and dust off the comet.

Comet Lovejoy in 2015

This comet's dust tail looks bright white, and the gas tail is colorful.

Parts of Comets

Comets have three main parts when they are close to the Sun. The nucleus is the solid middle part. The gas and dust cloud that is around the comet is the coma. The coma makes the nucleus hard to see from Earth.

The Sun pushes out the coma into long tails. Tails can be tens of millions of miles long. Comets often have a dust tail and a gas tail. When comets are far from the Sun, their ices stay frozen and they have no coma or tail.

Tails are not always behind the comet. The tails always point away from the Sun. When a comet is going toward the Sun, the tails are behind it. But the tails are in front of the comet when it is going away from the Sun.

The dust tail (*gray*) and gas tail (*blue*) always point away from the Sun.

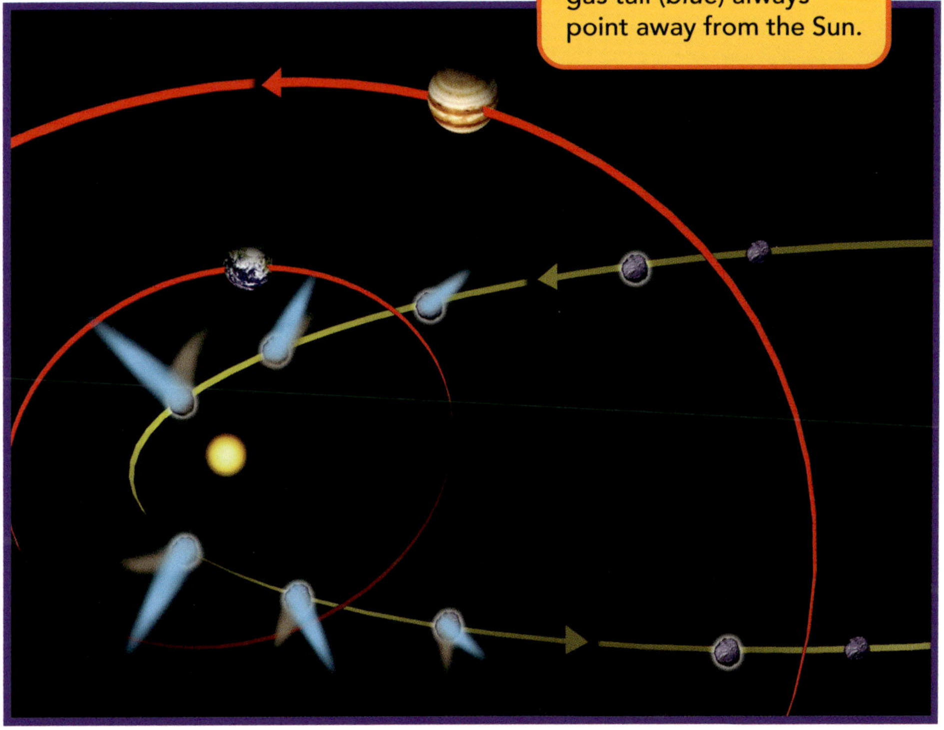

That's Not Right
TV and movies often show comets moving fast across the sky. This is wrong. Comets seen from Earth seem to move slowly through the sky from one night to the next.

Seeing Comets

Sometimes you can see comets in the night sky with telescopes or binoculars. Other times you can see them with just your eyes. That usually only happens every few years. The comets that we can see are often in the sky for a few weeks.

Comet NEOWISE in 2020

A woven image of Halley's Comet in 1066 CE

Halley's Comet in 1986

For thousands of years, people have drawn pictures of comets that they saw in the sky. People did not always know what comets were. Some people thought of comets as good or bad luck.

Halley's Comet is famous. It comes near the Sun and Earth about every seventy-five years. People have seen it for more than two thousand years. It will come near Earth again in 2061.

CHAPTER 4

EXPLORING COMETS

We have learned more about comets from spacecraft. Giotto explored Halley's Comet in 1986. It was the first time a spacecraft explored a comet.

Giotto found that Halley's Comet had different ices. These included water, carbon monoxide, and carbon dioxide ice. Giotto also took the first close-up pictures of a comet nucleus.

Halley's Comet as seen by Giotto in 1986

The Stardust mission brought the first comet samples to Earth. Stardust collected samples as it flew by Comet Wild 2 in 2004. In 2006, Stardust flew by Earth and dropped the samples for scientists to study.

Comet Wild 2 as seen in 2004

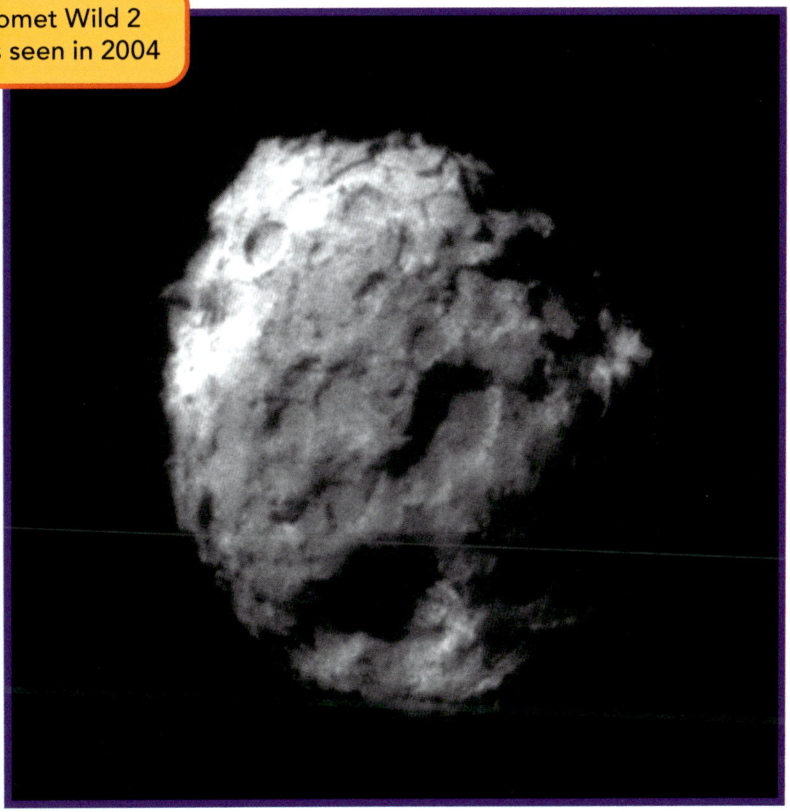

Naming Comets
Comets are usually named after the person or people who discovered them. That means comets may have more than one person's name.

Scientists sent the Deep Impact spacecraft to Comet Tempel 1 in 2005. They wanted to study what was beneath the surface of comets. A heavy ball slammed into the comet to dig up material. The spacecraft then studied the material.

Stardust did a flyby of Comet Tempel 1 in 2011. It studied the crater made by Deep Impact.

Comet Tempel 1 just after a heavy ball slammed into it at high speeds

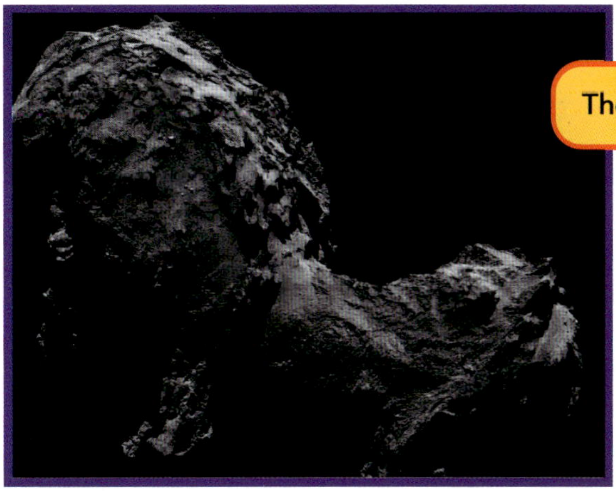

The nucleus of Comet 67P

The surface of Comet 67P

In 2014, the Rosetta spacecraft was the first to orbit a comet and drop a lander on a comet. It flew along with Comet 67P for almost two years as it got closer to the Sun. Rosetta was able to watch how the Sun's warmth changed the comet.

Future Missions

There will be many more asteroid spacecraft missions. They will show us new worlds. There will also likely be a comet for you to see. There's a lot to look forward to and enjoy with asteroids and comets!

This drawing shows the Psyche spacecraft arriving at a metal asteroid in 2029.

The 2021 launch of the Lucy spacecraft on its way to visit eleven asteroids

Glossary

asteroid: a rocky or metallic object in space, usually larger than 33 feet (10 m) wide and too small to become rounded due to self-gravity

atmosphere: the gases surrounding a planet, moon, or other body

comet: an icy, rocky object about the size of a city that spends most of its time far from the Sun and whose orbit brings it closer to the Sun

crater: a bowl-shaped hole caused by space rocks and other objects hitting the ground at high speeds

dwarf planet: a big, round, ball-shaped object that only goes around the Sun. Unlike a planet, it has one or more things close to the same size near its orbit.

orbit: the path a planet, moon, or other object follows as it goes around another object

planet: a big, round, ball-shaped object that only goes around the Sun. Our solar system has eight planets. A planet does not have anything close to the same size near its orbit.

spacecraft: a vehicle or object made for travel in outer space

Learn More

Betts, Bruce, PhD. *Dwarf Planets: Small Round Worlds*. Minneapolis: Lerner Publications, 2025.

Britannica Kids: Asteroid
https://kids.britannica.com/kids/article/asteroid/352796

Gladstone, James. *Journey around the Sun: The Story of Halley's Comet*. Berkeley, CA: Owlkids, 2021.

Kuchner, Marc J. *Asteroid vs. Comet*. Somerville, MA: MIT Kids, 2024.

NASA Space Place: What Is a Comet?
https://spaceplace.nasa.gov/comets/en/

The Planetary Society: Asteroids, Comets, and Other Small Worlds
https://www.planetary.org/worlds/asteroids-comets-small-worlds

Index

Photo Acknowledgments

Image credits: F. Scott Schafer/The Planetary Society, p. 2; Juan lacruz/Wikimedia Commons (PD), p. 4; NASA/JPL, pp. 6, 12; ESA/Hubble, M. Kornmesser, p. 7; NASA/JPL-Caltech/JAXA/ESA, p. 8; NASA/Goddard/SwRI/JHUAPL/NOIRLab/Wikimedia Commons (PD), p. 9 (top); NASA/Goddard/SwRI/JHUAPL/Wikimedia Commons (PD), p. 9 (bottom); Bruce Betts, p. 10; NASA/JSC/ANSMET, p. 11; NASA/JPL/JHUAPL, p. 13 (top); NASA/JHUAPL, p. 13 (bottom); JAXA/ISAS/Wikimedia Commons (PD), p. 14 (top); JAXA Hayabusa2/Wikimedia Commons (PD), p. 14 (bottom); NASA/JPL-Caltech/UCLA/MPS/DLR/IDA, p. 15 (top and bottom); NASA/Goddard/University of Arizona/Edited by The Planetary Society, p. 16 (top); NASA/Goddard/University of Arizona, p. 16 (bottom); NASA/processing by Eydeet Wikimedia Commons/Wikimedia Commons (PD), p. 17; NASA/Bill Dunford, p. 18; John Vermette/Wikimedia Commons (PD), p. 19; SimgDe/Wikimedia Commons (PD), p. 20; TIM BROWN/Science Source, p. 21; Rex Robichaux/Wikimedia Commons (PD), p. 22; Myrabella/Wikimedia Commons (PD), p. 23 (top); NASA/W. Liller/Wikimedia Commons (PD), p. 23 (bottom); ESA/MPS, p. 24; NASA/Wikimedia Commons (PD), p. 25; NASA/JPL-Caltech/UMD, p. 26; ESA/Rosetta/NAVCAM, p. 27 (top); ESA/Rosetta/MPS for OSIRIS Team MPS/UPD/LAM/IAA/SSO/INTA/UPM/DASP/IDA, p. 27 (bottom); NASA/JPL-Caltech/Arizona State Univ./Space Systems Loral/Peter Rubin, p. 28; NASA/Bill Ingalls, p. 29.
Cover: E. Kolmhofer, H. Raab; Johannes-Kepler-Observatory, Linz, Austria/Wikimedia Commons (PD).

For my sons, Daniel and Kevin, and for all the members of The Planetary Society®

Lerner Publications Company
An imprint of Lerner Publishing Group, Inc.
241 First Avenue North
Minneapolis, MN 55401 USA

For reading levels and more information, look up this title at www.lernerbooks.com.

Main body text set in Aptifer Sans LT Pro. Typeface provided by Linotype AG.

Editor: Angel Kidd **Designer:** Mary Ross **Photo Editor:** Angel Kidd

Library of Congress Cataloging-in-Publication Data

Names: Betts, Bruce (PhD), author.
Title: Asteroids and comets : orbiting space rocks / Bruce Betts, PhD.
Description: Minneapolis, MN : Lerner Publications, [2025] | Series: Exploring our solar system with the Planetary Society | Includes bibliographical references and index. | Audience: Ages 7–10 | Audience: Grades 2–3 | Summary: "Space is full of cool objects such as asteroids and comets. Readers will explore the rocky asteroid belt, icy Halley's Comet, and many other interesting space rocks and the spacecraft that study them"— Provided by publisher.
Identifiers: LCCN 2024012773 (print) | LCCN 2024012774 (ebook) | ISBN 9798765648315 (library binding) | ISBN 9798765661734 (paperback) | ISBN 9798765654590 (epub)
Subjects: LCSH: Asteroids—Juvenile literature. | Comets—Juvenile literature.
Classification: LCC QB651 .B48 2025 (print) | LCC QB651 (ebook) | DDC 523.44—dc23/eng/20240409

LC record available at https://lccn.loc.gov/2024012773
LC ebook record available at https://lccn.loc.gov/2024012774

Manufactured in the United States of America
1-1011036-53389-6/20/2024